For more information, please contact:

aquilla@adoregroup.co.uk

Published by Aquilla Books

Printed by Amazon.

First printing edition 2025.

Aquilla Books

Dedicated to the original door scratching kitty,
Kristoff. A cat whose best friend is a dog; a cat with
no boundaries, and zero respect for personal space,
but above all, a cat who has made our children laugh
every single day since we were chosen by him,
to be his family.

this book belongs to:

Kristoff

the Door Scratching Kitty

by

Donna Ostrom

Kristoff is a kitty,

He is black with four white paws.
He likes to cuddle, he loves to eat,
But his favourite thing
is scratching the doors.

In the middle of
each and every night,
When the house is fast asleep,
Kristoff knows what he wants to do,
And off to the hallway he creeps.

On quiet paws,
 he climbs the stairs,
and jumps over the baby gate.
He must reach the door on time,
He simply can't be late!

With a cry and a purr,
a miaow and a mew,
He sits up and flexes his claws:
And then he sets off to work...
By scratching at the doors!

He doesn't do it to cause trouble,
No, he's not a naughty boy.
He just wants to see his family
And to fill their hearts with joy.

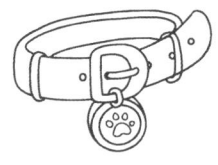

After he's done scratching,
He gives the door a few little bumps.
At last! It opens and he's in...
And on the bed he jumps.

With blurry eyes and sleepy yawns
And a scratch of their messy heads,
the children wonder what is
happening as they sit up in their beds.

And there he is, their little kitty,
So fluffy, cute and small.
Are they mad that he woke them up?
Of course not! Not at all!

the boy gives Kristoff a gentle pat.
the girl? She nuzzles his chin.
Kristoff is delighted,
His purrs cause quite the din!

Mum and dad,
they wake up too
And peek their heads around to see
the girl, the boy and Kristoff
Cuddling up
(with the occasional flea).

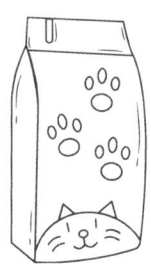

And there they rest,
the three best friends,
As they lay back down
in a snuggly heap,
It isn't long before they
close their eyes
And drift back off to sleep.

the end.

Also by Donna Ostrom:

Mongoose Betty

Scan the QR code to find out more

Aquilla Books

Published by Aquilla Books

Where Stories Are Crafted with Purpose and Told with Pride

For more information, email:

aquilla@adoregroup.co.uk

Printed in Dunstable, United Kingdom

68738668R00018

Escape from the Maze

by Narinder Dhami

illustrated by Sarah Jennings

OXFORD
UNIVERSITY PRESS

Eve was having a day out. She was with her mother and her brother, Paul.

They were visiting some wonderful gardens.

Eve spotted something across the gardens. "Look, Mum! A maze!" she said.

The maze was constructed of tall, green bushes. They were planted very close to each other.

"I could easily find my way out of there!" Eve declared confidently.

Her mother smiled. "Let's go in," she said.

They walked to the start of the maze.

"There's Sonny from your class, Eve," Mum said.

"Oh no!" Eve sighed. "He's so quiet and boring!"

Sonny was with his grandmother.

"Look, Sonny, there's Eve from school," Gran said.

Sonny stared at Eve with dislike.
"She talks too loudly," he muttered.
"She hurts my ears!"

Eve glared at him. "I heard that!"
she snapped.

Sonny said nothing and looked away.

"Let's see who escapes the maze first," Eve shouted. "Race you!"

Sonny frowned. He was worried about going into the maze. However, he didn't want Eve to win.

Sonny nodded.

Eve dashed into the maze. Her mother hurried after her.

Sonny walked in behind them. He stopped, looking all around him.

"I must study everything carefully, Gran," Sonny explained.

Meanwhile, Eve had raced confidently ahead of him. "It's this way, Mum!" she shouted.

Then Eve skidded to a halt. "This is a dead end!" she cried.

"Let's try another way," her mother said.

"This way, Gran," Sonny said.

"Didn't we just come that way?" asked Gran.

"No, the leaves look different," Sonny replied.

"But all the leaves look the same!"
Gran sighed.

Eve was still sprinting around the maze at top speed.

"Another dead end!" she wailed.

Paul started crying.

"Here, Paul, have a pear," Mum said.
"Where now, Eve?"

"I'm not sure," Eve muttered.

Sonny hoped he was on the right track.
It was taking so long! Now he was worried.
Maybe Eve had already won?

Eve was feeling very frustrated. She was worried, too. Maybe Sonny had already found the way out?

Just then, Eve and Sonny bumped into each other!

"Gran and I are lost!" Sonny blurted out.

"So are we," Eve admitted. "Let's team up. We can ask for some help."

Sonny watched as Eve spoke to a group
of children. He was impressed! Eve was so
confident and friendly.

"They said that way is a dead end," Eve explained.

Eve and Sonny walked the other way. Then they came to another fork in the path.

"Let's go left," Eve said.

"No, we should go right," Sonny said. "Look at these wet footprints. Lots of people have come back from the left fork. It must be a dead end."

"Well spotted!" Eve said.

They walked to the right.

"I think the maze is leading us to the coffee shop," Sonny said.

"So we must turn here," Eve agreed.

A few moments later, they saw the exit. Eve and Sonny grinned at each other.

"We can tell everyone at school how we escaped the maze together!" Eve said.

Can You Escape?

Find your way out of the maze like Eve and Sonny did!

Encourage the child to follow the path and find their way out of the maze.